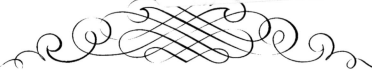

ISBN 978-1-331-75815-0
PIBN 10230855

This book is a reproduction of an important historical work. Forgotten Books uses
state-of-the-art technology to digitally reconstruct the work, preserving the original format
whilst repairing imperfections present in the aged copy. In rare cases, an imperfection in
the original, such as a blemish or missing page, may be replicated in our edition. We do,
however, repair the vast majority of imperfections successfully; any imperfections that
remain are intentionally left to preserve the state of such historical works.

1 MONTH OF
FREE
READING

at

www.ForgottenBooks.com

By purchasing this book you are eligible for one month membership to ForgottenBooks.com, giving you unlimited access to our entire collection of over 700,000 titles via our web site and mobile apps.

To claim your free month visit:

www.forgottenbooks.com/free230855

Similar Books Are Available from
www.forgottenbooks.com

JOHN STEWART

Missionary to the Wyandots

REV. N. B. C. LOVE, D.D.

THE MISSIONARY SOCIETY OF THE METHODIST
EPISCOPAL CHURCH
RINDGE LITERATURE DEPARTMENT
150 FIFTH AVENUE, NEW YORK

PRICE FIVE CENTS

JOHN STEWART

Pioneer Missionary of the Methodist Episcopal Church

By N. B. C. Love, D.D.

The Methodist Episcopal Church from its organization in 1773 was missionary in its spirit. It made continuous efforts towards the conversion of the whites and blacks, but the red men of the forest were passed by. The minutes of the annual conferences, at the beginning of the last century, reported in separate columns the numbers of whites and blacks in each society, but no figures for the Indians.

The Methodist Episcopal Church was aggressive in the older States and passed into the Northwest Territory and the greater West and South. In the providence of God John Stewart was the apostle to the heathen Wyandots, and the founder of the first Methodist Episcopal Mission among the heathen.

" BETWEEN-THE-LOGS."

Before the advent of Stewart the most cruel and bloody practices obtained among the Wyandots. In this respect they were not different from the other Indian tribes of the Northwest. The burning of Col. Crawford, when a prisoner, is evidence of this. Even the women and children participated in torturing him. We need not repeat the story here. The Wyandots were the leaders in this savage deed. Between-the-Logs, it is claimed, was a participant, and such

An Apostle to the Wyandots

were the people to whom Stewart carried the gospel of love and peace.

The Wyandots for a long period stood politically at the head of an Indian Federation of tribes and so were recognized by the United States Government in the treaties made with the Indians of the old Northwest Territory.

The names of chiefs of the Wyandot nation appear first and prominently on the treaty made at Greenville in 1795 between the Government and the Indians, Gen. Wayne acting for our Government.

Co-operation of two Bishops While the itinerant Bishops Asbury and McKendree and their worthy helpers were denied the honor of inaugurating the great missionary movement among the heathen, they are to be honored for their unselfishness in giving their co-operation and support to John Stewart, an humble mulatto layman, who had been converted through their preaching, and whom they recognized as having received the call of God.

John Stewart's parents were free people of color who resided in Powhattan County, Va. They were Baptists, and of good repute. John went to winter school while a boy at home, and was more favored in this than many negro boys. While in his early manhood he learned the dyer's trade and earned some money, but a highwayman robbed him of all. The fear of destitution worried him, for he felt that to be poor was to be in disgrace, and he purposed to commit suicide. Hesitating in this, he drank intoxicants to drown his sorrow, until a kind Christian friend persuaded him to desist and reform. Although failing several times in his efforts, he at last succeeded.

Stewart's Conversion He listened to the preaching of the Gospel by the Methodists and was converted. Finding no Baptist Society convenient, he united with the Methodist Episcopal Church. Here he was at home. The prayer and class meeting were delightful to him, and all his prejudices against the Methodists gave way. He also prospered in business and saved some money. The grandfather of Bishop McCabe was his class leader and personal friend.

Stewart has been described to me by two pioneers who knew him well. He was a light mulatto, about five feet, eight inches high, weighing about one hundred and forty pounds; well formed, erect in carriage, easy and graceful in movement. His features were more European than African. He had a tenor voice, and was gifted in song.

He often went into the fields or forests to meditate, to study the Bible and to pray. One Sabbath evening he was in the edge of the woods by the side of a rivulet that ran into the Ohio, when a voice from the sky seemed to say to him in audible tone, " Thou shalt go to the Northwest and declare my counsel plainly." As he listened and looked, a peculiar halo appeared to fill the Western sky. This summons was repeated. The first was in the voice of a man, the second that of a woman. That he was honest in the thought of this calling there need be no doubt.

A deep impression was made on his astonished mind. He had no thought of preaching; he felt he would obey fully by teaching and exhorting, but when a friend told him he was called to preach he rebelled, feeling he was not prepared nor worthy. He resolved to go to Tennessee, but sickness came to him, and for awhile his life was despaired of, but finally recovering, the impression that it was his duty to go to the Northwest was intensified.

The Northwest, beyond a fringe of settlements, was a vast illimitable wilderness, occupied by savage beasts and as savage men. He resolved to go, not for gain, nor for fame, nor for pleasure, but to save souls from the bondage of heathen darkness. The risks were many, but he felt that an unseen hand was over him. Starting on his journey, he knew not whither he went any more than Abraham of old. His friends tried to persuade him not to go, and having started, those whom he met in the settlements also tried such persuasion, or laughed

A Summons to Service

A Journey into the Wilderness

JOHN STEWART LISTENING TO THE "VOICE" WHICH
CALLED HIM TO PREACH TO THE WYANDOTS.
From a painting by Rev. N. B. C. Love, D.D.

at his folly, but to no purpose. The red men of the forest, neglected by the Government and despised, feared and hated by the frontiersmen, were upon his mind. He believed they were dear to the heart of Jesus.

He went on, keeping towards the Northwest, wading streams, camping alone at night, unarmed in the primeval forests, enduring hunger and many other hardships. After the severe toil of days and exposure of nights, he came to the village of the Delawares — on the headwaters of the Sandusky River. The Indians extended to him the hospitality of their cabins. Here he held religious worship, singing, praying and telling the story of the dying love of Jesus until late at night, then, retiring, he fell asleep, feeling that his mission was accomplished and that he would start on his homeward journey in a day of two. With the dawn of the morning, however, he awoke and heard an inward voice telling him to go farther. Having inquired the way, he started again on his pilgrimage.

The first afternoon he came to the cabin of a white family and was refused admittance by the wife until the return of her husband. Upon the husband's arrival, while supper was preparing, Stewart sang some sweet songs, which charmed the backwoodsman and his family. He offered to hold services at night, and the boys were sent post haste by the father to the few residents in the vicinity. Stewart had about a dozen in his congregation to whom he expounded the Gospel, and sang Methodist hymns, to their great entertainment. The Divine Spirit was in the word and several were awakened and saved. Among the number was the daughters of the home in which he was entertained. He tarried for several days, holding services at night and forming a class.

In a few days he found himself in Upper Sandusky, an entire stranger, without an introduction to any one. He called at the home of William Walker, sub-Indian agent, who thought him a fugitive from Slavery, but Stewart in a sincere, artless manner gave his history,

A Backwoods
Congregation

including his Christian experience. Mr. Walker was convinced, and gave him words of encouragement, directing him to the cabin of Jonathan Pointer.

A Providential Helper

Pointer was a black man who had been stolen by the Wyandots when he was a child. He could converse fluently in both the English and Wyandot languages. Here was a providential helper in opening an "effectual door" to the Divinely appointed missionary of the Methodist Episcopal Church.

Pointer was not favorably impressed with Stewart, and tried to dissuade him from his undertaking by telling him of the efforts of the Roman Catholic missionaries and their complete failure. He did not know that "the kingdom of heaven cometh not by observation." Indeed, Jonathan Pointer was as much a heathen as the Wyandots, and was at that time preparing to participate in an Indian dance and religious feast. Stewart wanted to accompany him, and Jonathan reluctantly consented. Stewart as a visitor sat in silence and witnessed the dance. When an interval of rest occurred, he asked the privilege of addressing them on the purpose of his visit which, with their consent, he did, Jonothan interpreting and rather enjoying the notoriety it gave him.

An Audience of Indian Warriors

Here was a scene worthy the brush of the artist. The first heathen audience of hundreds of Indian warriors in war paint and gaudy costumes listening to a messenger of the Methodist Episcopal Church; Jonathan, too, in paint and feathers, while a mild-mannered mulatto told them the purpose of his visit. Here was Christian courage equal to that of Fr. Marquette or any of the old Jesuit Fathers of the Roman Catholic Church. In this Stewart evinced extraordinary courage and faith in the Heavenly Father.

At the conclusion of his address he invited all to shake hands with him, and on motion of Chief Bloody Eyes, all passed by in single file and did so. An appointment was made at Jonathan's cabin for the next evening, and by the light of the cabin fire Stewart preached his first sermon. This was late in November, 1816.

Stewart met the Wyandots daily, Jonathan interpreting and saying: "What Stewart says may be true,
he did not know, he only translated fairly." Many were
greatly interested and a few awakened. The efforts of
Stewart to secure the conversion of his interpreter were
unceasing, and his reward soon came in an open pro-
fession on the part of Jonathan, who became a firm, out-
spoken believer. The soil of his jovial African heart

**REV. JAMES B. FINLEY PREACHING TO THE WYANDOT
INDIANS AT UPPER SANDUSKY.**
The black man, Jonathan Pointer, interpreting.

was thin and did not bring forth perfect and matured
fruit. He was naturally vain and sometimes was given
to drink, but God used him as one of "the foolish things
of this world to confound the wise." He was demonstra-
tively pious in church.

The missionary met with opposition from the whites
who sold "fire water" to the Indians. They maligned
him, persecuted and tried to scare him away: They
said, "he was no minister, a fraud, a villain," and some
of the leading chiefs became his enemies. Dark days

had come. The muttering of a storm was heard, but nothing daunted, Stewart sang, prayed, and going from cabin to cabin found those who received him and his words gladly. The agent, William Walker, Jonathan and a few other leaders were his friends. Indians prejudiced by Catholic teaching joined the opposition. His Bible, they said, "is not the true Bible," but these questions being left to Mr. Walker, the decision was favorable to John Stewart. Walker said there was little difference between the Catholic and Protestant Bibles, one being a translation from the Latin, the other from the Greek and Hebrew, and both from the same original documents; and that any layman called of God had the divine right to preach and teach. Thus through this layman and Government officer, Stewart was helped in his work.

Superstitious Savages The Wyandots were superstitious, believing in magic, witchcraft, religious dancing and feasting. These things Stewart opposed with Scripture and reason, and gave any who desired the opportunity to defend them. John Hicks, a chief, undertook this. "These things," he said, "are part of the religion of our forefathers handed down from ancient times, and the Great Spirit was the author of them, and all nations have religions given them, the same being adapted to their needs."

Mononcue, then a heathen, endorsed what Hicks said. He also said, "The Bible is the white man's book and Jesus the white man's teacher; they were sent first to white men, why not to the Indians?"

Stewart said, "In the beginning Jesus commissioned his disciples saying, 'Go ye into all the world and preach the Gospel to every creature.' This is as much for you as for any others; we bring His Gospel to you and if you receive it not you shall be damned. The Bible is for all. Christ died for all that all might be saved."

First Converts among the Indians Stewart continued and Mononcue, Hicks and others were convicted and converted. Many others embraced the truth. These were among his first converts. Having

10

never been Roman Catholics, their prejudices were easy to overcome.

Crowds came to Stewart's meetings nightly, and the work of revival increased. Many of the younger converts became, under the leadership of Stewart, good singers. Stewart's solo singing was a special attraction to the unbelievers. He always sang with the spirit and with the understanding also. While he was not demonstrative nor vociferous, he had the gift of persuasion and could logically impress the truth on other minds. He was not a scholar, but he had a good common school education and upon this foundation, through his intercourse with books, nature and God he became an efficient workman. Several of his sermons found in print, although not fully reported, evince the fact that he had clear conceptions of theology, especially as relates to man as a sinner, and a sinner to be saved by Grace.

In February, 1817, Stewart felt that something more radical must be done in order to bring about the conversion of those who were under his instruction. Their convictions were more of the head than of the heart. He and those with him prayed daily for the outpouring of the Holy Spirit, and their prayer was granted. Revival power came upon these heathen, and there was deep and pungent conviction for sins and real conversions. This work of grace aroused opposition. Deep Convictions and Real Conversions

The heathen party arranged for a "Thanksgiving Feast and Dance." It was for the whole Wyandot nation, and so Stewart and his followers attended. Stewart went with misgivings; he simply sat and looked on. To his surprise his converts joined in the dance, Mononcue with others. Stewart had protested against this, and he went away discouraged, resolving to leave them. He announced his purpose and preached his farewell sermon the next Sunday from Acts 20:30. This sermon, reported and printed by William Walker, the writer has read. Earnestly Stewart plead with the converts to avoid all heathen practices, and warned the heathen present, kindly but earnestly, to flee from the wrath to come.

He narrated his call to come to them and his labors with them, and told them they should see his face no more. There was general weeping, even the heathen joining in the lamentation. Stewart then addressed the chiefs and principal men, while silence reigned among the large audience assembled in the council house, as he bade all good bye.

Stewart Returns to Marietta On the suggestion of Mrs. Warpole, a collection was taken for Stewart, amounting to ten dollars. He left and returned to Marietta. A few remained faithful. Heathenism and drunkenness held full sway. Only twenty men of the Wyandot nation did not drink intoxicants. Although Stewart was away his heart was with the Indians and after only a few months, to the joy of the Christian Indians, he returned. During his absence he wrote an excellent pastoral letter to the little flock. Throughout, his spirit and conduct evinced the unselfishness of his motives.

With his return came an increase of zeal, and power and increased success crowned his efforts. The work enlarged. It was more than Stewart was able to do. A prominent Methodist minister of another denomination than the Episcopal Methodists, visited him and tried to have him change his relationship, but it was of no avail. He sent an account of " The Lord's doings " among the Wyandots to a session of the Ohio Annual Conference and asked for a helper who could assist him in preaching and administration.

A List of Missionaries As nearly as can be ascertained, the names of the missionaries and time are: John Stewart, 1816 to 1823; James Montgomery, 1819; Moses Henkle, 1820; J. B. Finley, 1821 to 1827 — part of this time as presiding elder; Charles Elliot, 1822; Jacob Hooper, 1823; J. C. Brook, 1825; James Gilruth, 1826-27; Russell Bigelow served as junior missionary in 1827 and in 1828 was in charge of the mission and of the district as presiding elder with Thomas Thompson, junior missionary; B. Boydson, 1830; E. C. Gavitt, 1831; Thomas Simms, 1832; S. P. Shaw, 1835; S. M. Allen, 1837; James Wheeler, 1839-1843; Ralph Wilcox, 1843.

The teachers in the mission were: Miss Harriett Stubbs, Miss Margaret Hooper, Liberty Prentis, Miss E. A. Gibbs, Asbury Sabin, Jane Parker, matron, and teacher of spinning, weaving and domestic work, Mrs. Jane Riley, L. M. Pounds and the missionaries' wives.

Up to this time Stewart was an exhorter, his license being signed by Father McCabe, grandfather of Bishop Charles C. McCabe. The license was given while Stewart was in Marietta.

He now attended a Quarterly Meeting on Mad River Circuit. Bishop George was present and presided. "After a careful examination, John Stewart was licensed as a local preacher." **A Local Preacher's License**

With money raised by Bishop McKendree a tract of fifty-three acres of land on the east side of the Sandusky, near Harmen's Mill, was bought for Stewart. About this time Bishop McKendree, in feeble health, came to the mission on horseback, from Lancaster, Ohio, and was accompanied by J. B. Finley and D. J. Soul, Jr. The Bishop was delighted to find "the Lord had a people among the Wyandots."

The money paid for the land was collected by Bishop McKendree at camp meetings and conferences. In this is not only an official recognition but a memorial of the large heartedness of this pioneer Bishop.

About 1820 Stewart married Polly, a mulatto girl. She was a devout Christian, and could read and write. With her he lived in his own cabin home and with the help of his wife and friends soon had enough from the virgin soil, with some money assistance from the conference, to live in pioneer comfort. **Marriage and Home Life**

Near the end of 1823, after a battle with consumption, the word spread among the Christians that Stewart was dying; a number of Christian chiefs and devout men and women were with him. Christmas and the New Year were at hand. Stewart calmly exhorted all — told how the Lord sustained him, and gave his testimony to the power of Christ to save. Holding his wife's hand, he said to all, "Oh, be faithful," and died. In an **Stewart's Death** humble grave on his land he was buried, and for twenty years thereafter no stone marked his resting-place.

But he was not forgotten. His grave was often visited, and the Indian youth were taught to place flowers on his grave each spring and summer time.

In 1843 the Rev. James Wheeler, missionary, just before the Indians left for the West, had Stewart's remains taken up and reinterred at the southeast corner

REV. N. B. C. LOVE, D.D.

of the "old mission," and a free stone slab placed at his head with a suitable epitaph.

This church was erected in 1824, the money, $1,333.33, being donated by the Government through Hon. J. C. Calhoun, Secretary of War. Rev. J. B. Findley was the instigator in securing this, and he was made the custodian of the money pending its disposition in the erection of this church. The building later went into decay, and the gravestones were carried away piece-

14

WYANDOT MISSION CHURCH IN RUINS, UPPER SANDUSKY, OHIO, 1884.

meal by relic hunters, until in 1886 all vestige of them was gone. A similar condition of affairs pertained with reference to the wood work and the furnishings of the Mission Church.

The Mission Restored In 1860 and 61 when these were in a fair state of preservation, the writer, then a young man in his first station, Upper Sandusky, made a chart and diagram of the church and cemetery, the location of the buried dead, with copies of the epitaphs on each tombstone, which he preserved. The work of restoration was done with money — $2,000 — donated by the Missionary Society of M. E. Church, by order of the General Conference. The writer, as chairman of the restoration committee, had the honor of using this money in erecting once again, out of its ruins, the first mission church of Episcopal Methodism, and the first Protestant mission church in the Northwest Territory. When Charles Elliott was missionary, a log building was erected in which Stewart, Elliott and others preached, and here Harriett Stubbs taught the children. It was a temporary log building and, so far as we know, was not used exclusively as a church, and was not dedicated.

Rededication During the session of the Central Ohio Annual Conference in September, 1889, the restored Mission Church was rededicated. There were several thousand more people present than could get into the house, so the services were held under the old oak trees which had sheltered the hundreds of Wyandots who had worshiped in the church.

Dr. Adam C. Barnes, P.E., was chairman. Dr. P. P. Pope, grandson of Russell Bigelow, led in prayer. Addresses were delivered by Bishop J. F. Hurst, Hon. D. D. Hare, Dr. L. A. Belt, Gen. W. H. Gibson, a historical address by the writer, and reminiscences by Dr. E. C. Gavitt, only surviving missionary, and a hymn in Wyandot sung by "Mother Solomon," a member in her childhood of the first mission school. Many were present whose parents or grandparents had been connected in some way with the mission.

WYANDOT MISSION CHURCH, RESTORED, 1889.

The name and work of John Stewart is perpetuated in this restored and really monumental church, in the engraved marble tablet in its walls, the granite marking his grave, and in each mission church and mission school of Episcopal Methodism throughout the world.

The good work inaugurated by this humble but excellent Christian character will never be forgotten, but as the ages come and go, and the heathen world is brought to Christ, his name shall be more remembered and honored. All admit that his success among the Wyandots led to the organization of the Missionary Society of the Methodist Episcopal Church in 1819. And was not the mission school at Upper Sandusky the genesis of the Woman's Foreign Missionary work? If so, then all honor to Harriett Stubbs and Jane Parker and their worthy successors.

"MOTHER SOLOMON."

Let the name of Stewart be placed in the list of the world's benefactors. May his sublime faith, clear conviction of the Divine presence, enthusiasm, endurance, patience and unselfishness, awaken in the hearts of each reader of these pages the spirit of emulation.

CPSIA information can be obtained at www.ICGtesting.com
Printed in the USA
BVOW05s1956310116

434952BV00020B/753/P